Dog Owners:
A Spotter's Guide

Robbie Guillory

Illustrations by Judith Hastie

FREIGHT BOOKS

First published 2015

Freight Books
49-53 Virginia Street
Glasgow, G1 1TS
www.freightbooks.co.uk

A CIP catalogue reference for this book is available from the British Library.
ISBN 978-1-910449-39-4
eISBN 978-1-910449-40-0

Typeset by Freight
Printed and bound by Bell and Bain, Glasgow

Contents

Utilitarian Group *Useful or practical rather than attractive*

Over-Working Group *Harassed by life's many problems*

Toy Group *Just want to be played with*

Crossbreed Group *Are they even proper Owners at all?*

On Spotting Dog Owners

In the age of automation, when modern society has leisure time
undreamed of by our forebears, it's an important part of a healthy lifestyle
to have a past-time that takes us outside, into the fresh air, to engage with
the natural world, regardless of where we live. 'Spotting' is becoming
increasingly popular in towns, cities and rural parts across the nation,
as was evidenced by the huge success of my previous study, *Cyclists: a
spotter's guide*. So in order to pay for moat cleaning and a new duck island,
I've decided to share another hugely rewarding category of Spotting: the
humble Dog Owner.

   Dog Ownership, in the modern sense, originated in the nineteenth
century in the United Kingdom (for my American readers, that place with
the lady who wears the funny, twinkly hat and lives in a castle, near that bit
in the middle of the map call 'Europe'). 1873 saw the establishment of the
Collared Club of which I am Secretary (NB: not to be mistaken with the
Collar Club, a society founded at Oxford in 1912 dedicated to the practise
and promotion of sado-masochism, an organisation of which our dear
Prime Minister and Chancellor of the Exchequer are both active members).
However this formalisation had more to do with the Victorians' obsessive
need to categorise and catalogue rather than the actual birth of Dog
Ownership.

   Historians and archaeologists (another wonderful, if narrow, category
for Spotting…) have presented compelling evidence of Dog Ownership
dating back to Neolithic times. The club or cudgel seen in the hands of our
ancestors in cave art is now known to have been a stick for throwing. And
there is overwhelming evidence that Stonehenge, that jewel in the crown of
ancient monuments, was not a ceremonial site but was actually designed

and built for agility classes.

Egypt provides the most conclusive evidence of dog ownership in the ancient world. Academia is now unanimous in its belief that representations of Anubis, the figure who is half dog, half man, isn't a deity but merely a shorthand symbol of owning a pooch. And radical theories are now circulating that the pyramids were not burial chambers but huge, monumental celebrations of the perfectly excreted dog poo, which the Ancient Egyptians are alleged to have worshipped.

Furthermore, studies of the protrusions on the helmets of Vikings have proved, beyond a shadow of a doubt, that they were not horns or wings (as favoured in performances of Wagner operas) but pointy ears, to easily mark out in battle Viking men who had undertaken the important rite-of-passage of becoming a Dog Owner, greatly adding, they believed, to their masculinity and fighting prowess.

If you take the time to look, you'll discover that Dog Owners are to be found in every part of this land and in most countries beyond. They are ubiquitous. Some might say rife. They can be found pacing the streets in the early morning and late at night, gathering in the parks and on canal tow-paths. Mountains and beaches are other favourites, possibly congregation points from where they migrate to the annual rutting known as 'Crufts' (or on the North American continent, 'Westminster').

What is the pleasure in Spotting Dog Owners, rather than other popular categories like, say, Car Drivers, Internet Daters or the aforementioned Cyclists? For me it's their remarkable compulsion to take canines as pets that's long fascinated me. This is the easiest way for a beginner to identify a Dog Owner, distinct from Cat and Budgie Owners or almost mythical rarities like Iguana and Alpaca Owners. Important basic distinctions exist between Owners that are 'with lead', 'without lead' or using the confusing 'extendable lead' (often invisible from distance, the extendable lead is most identifiable by the regular yanking motion displayed by the Owner when the pet strays out of a three metre 'safety zone' or looks like it's found some tasty vomit to eat).

For those who aspire to intermediate or advanced Spotting, great pleasures lie ahead. Observing the way an Owner communes with his dog – whether he be grooming, playing or feeding – is a true marvel. Owner habits are in constant flux, too, influenced by a range of factors such as social status, climate and fashion. For instance, in the last ten to fifteen years in my own country, Owners have started to collect their dogs' faeces in small plastic bags, a practise that originated in California around forty years ago where Owners evolved something called a 'pooper-scooper', now a rarity and much prized by advanced Spotters. Poo or Poop bags are of great importance to Owners (Owners who are bagless lose status amongst others of their kind). Bags are used to build monuments, known as cairns, usually in or beside bins. They are also thrown into bushes or over walls in displays of bravura, and sometimes are even thrown into neighbours' gardens as a sign of deep affection and respect.

Some more advice for beginners. The best way to work out what breed of Owner you have spotted is to first identify their dog, as there is truth in the adage that dogs invariably absorb the identifying characteristics of the Owner through a symbiotic osmosis known as 'companionship'. Never think, however, that there's only one specific breed of dog for every breed of Owner. You're just as likely to see an adult Red Trouser with a chocolate Labrador as with a muddy Spaniel. Owners, you'll observe, are highly acquisitive and often indiscriminate in dog selection.

For evidence of this locate the gathering place known as the 'rescue centre' where distraught Owners who've misplaced a pet are given special mongrel dogs called 'broken toys', identifiable as such by repetitive jumping, barking, whining, biting and leg-humping. Other example contradictions include The Boomerang, which is nothing like its Dog in temperament, while you are highly unlikely to see a Broken Athlete with anything other than a Greyhound. Such are the subtle complexities that make Spotting Dog Owners such a pleasure.

In addition to dog identification, beginners will soon discover it's the attitude and personality of an Owner that will unlock the secrets to its breed. Careful observation of coat, colour and, most importantly, behaviour is the essential weapon in the Spotter's armoury. And don't think you'll spot them all in a year or two. Some are very rare, restricted to remotest, most inhospitable, god-forsaken parts of the British Isles, like Scotland or North Wales, for God's sake

The venerable Collared Club has been in existence for nearly 150 years, documenting and standardising all the different breeds contained in this book, a vitally important task in preserving and enhancing this valuable part of our national ecology. We're extremely proud to have exported the art of Dog Spotting abroad through the Great British Empire, although understandably in countries with less rigorous management of breeds, there is much confusion between classes through the indiscriminate cross-breeding of Owners.

But here in the UK our Club has been proud custodian of a species that gives great pleasure – whilst even performing useful tasks (see for example the Over-working Group) – and it's been our aim to save Owner breeds from deviating from their ideal. Best of luck with your spotting. I hope this book gives you an appreciation of the beauty and diversity of the Dog Owner and aids you in embracing the wonderful activity of Owner Spotting.

Guide to the Guide

It has been seventy-five years since the Collared Club produced the last edition of *Dog Owners: a spotter's guide*. Much too long a gap, you might say… but we were never an organisation for innovation, rather one dedicated to preserving the status quo.

However, a new, revised and updated edition is clearly a necessity in a time of great change. Varieties of Dog Owner have exploded, to a point where we have been required to even include a section on that dreaded modern phenomenon, the Crossbreed. Undoubtedly controversial – heretical for some, even – the Club committee have nonetheless decided by a narrow majority to look beyond our aging core membership towards what's popular amongst other demographics (with large amounts of disposable income).

That bastion of radical liberalism, the *Daily Mail*, recently asked 'Has the Collared Club gone barking mad!?', and it took the author some time to be persuaded that this was a justifiable move. However, moat cleaning and duck islands won't pay for themselves…

There are in the region of 8 million Dog Owners in the UK today; a vast increase on the 5 million recorded in 1970, which was at the time seen as an unassailable figure. Of these Dog Owners, we have identified some forty-two breeds, and there are countless sub-types too. Each breed has a descriptive standard, most of which were laid out when the Club was founded, and every year we see marvellous examples appear at Chumps, our annual gathering. Changes have been made, however. In a bid to rectify past mistakes we have removed descriptions now known to be detrimental to the well-being of Owners. These may have encouraged misunderstanding of behaviour at best and mistreatment at worst.

We have also taken the opportunity to refresh the illustrations of Dog Owners, as the Club feels that the breeds have moved on from those depicted by Sir Edwin Landseer when our Club was founded. The changes are, in some places, significant. For instance, the eponymous Red Trouser is in decline, and has developed a far whiter head of hair than the ruddy-faced youth shown by Landseer in the first edition. Our images have been produced by famed animal portraitist Judith Hastie, who has cemented a career with her illustrations of dogs, Kindle users, cyclists and 'Jocks'.

Finally, mention must be made to the geographical nature of the breeds found here. This is a book of British Dog Owners exclusively. Other types are found across the European continent and beyond, but we have not covered those we would class as being 'exotic', such as the Shits-On-You or Maltese Crossdresser. There are many books that cover these more colourful breeds, such as Grooming von Parlour's definitive 12 volume *Hundebesitzer from the Algarve to the Russian Steppe.*

Gamekeeper

The name Gamekeeper is derived from the strange fascination this breed has with wild animals and birds, especially pheasants. You will often see him feeding adult birds, or tending to young clutches of chicks. He's highly territorial and fiercely protective of all living creatures within his ranging area (with the exception of raptors who he despises), often threatening violence against anyone that approaches or 'disturbs the cover' unless specifically paid to do so. We strongly advise Spotters to keep their distance and observe only through a strong pair of field glasses.

Because of his affection for the pheasant, grouse and partridge, many Gamekeepers are kept on the large shooting estates (one of the few breeds to have been, if not domesticated, then at least tamed by mankind), where he does a tremendous job for very little upkeep (a small amount of money, a kennel known as a 'tied-cottage' and a bottle of spirits at Christmas) though he does have to be confined to a cage when the shoot actually commences.

This Dog Owner is capable of working tirelessly all day, ready to enter water even when he must break ice to do so. His thick coat is tough and weather resistant (so long as he's 'waxed' in the Spring each year), which is handy as he's known to sleep under hedges when he's had too many whiskies. In the East of England you may see a Gamekeeper sporting a bowler hat, which he cleverly makes from river mud and moleskins. Hair and beard need to be kept well-trimmed if he's not to suffer from uninvited seeds, twigs and scrambled egg getting caught, causing great distress. The Gamekeeper has a language, of sorts, though it's largely unintelligible.

Dog – Border Terrier or Jack Russell, the rattier the better.

General Appearance – Well-built, compact, strong, merry and active.

Characteristics – This breed is of ancient and pure origins, and may once, before civilization reached these shores, have played a vital role in the ecosystem as the only natural predator of the Poacher.

Temperament – Friendly, happy disposition, especially when 'three sheets to the wind'. Can become thunderous when drunk, or when under the impression his wards are at risk. Timidity is highly undesirable in pups.

Body – Strong, neither too long nor too short. Chest deep, well developed. Legs slightly bowed, but not unduly so. Hands should be large, yet capable of great gentleness.

Gait/Movement – Legs swing straight from the hip, throwing feet well forward in an easy manner. Makes very little noise. A strong movement, able to be kept up for many miles.

Faults – Look out for alcoholism and membership of the paramilitary wing of the Countryside Alliance.

Most Likely to Own – nothing other than a hipflask. All other accoutrements are borrowed from the Red Trouser, towards whom the Gamekeeper is deferential while working but contemptuous of in private.

Red Trouser

The Red Trouser, distinguished above all by its scarlet legs and tweedy coat, is a real gentleman, who adores children and has a kind and loving nature, except when threatened by 'Pinkos'. Due to the continuing disintegration of his natural habitat – large country estates – he's sadly in decline and you are more likely to see an older specimen walking with his dog round the local town on market day, than a younger example in his natural habitat. A country squire at heart, the city not really his scene, the Red Trouser comes alive in the countryside, talking loudly at – but not listening to – other breeds such as the Farming Subsidy and Gamekeeper.

An avid fisherman, the Red Trouser is thought to have evolved along the banks of Britain's world-famous salmon rivers, though he's not above having a pop at a grouse or two should he be led to them by a Gamekeeper.

Dog – retrievers such as disobedient, overweight Labradors in any colour (although darker shades are more common), hyperactive Cocker or Springer Spaniels or any other breed deemed suitably 'country'.

General Appearance – In youth, ruddy cheeks to match his legs, and in old age a shock of white or sandy hair and marked by a fine line of bristles following the top of his muzzle, though the rest of his face should be as smooth at a baby's bottom. The Red Trouser should be strongly built, and very active.

Characteristics – Good-tempered, with a keen love of water (or at least what swims in it). A devoted companion and generous host. Prone to occasional barking at the television or radio.

Temperament – Intelligent and keen, with a strong will to please, the result of a youth spent at boarding school, where he remained dogless until long after puberty due to Matron's intolerance of pets. The Red Trouser should display above all a kindly nature, with little aggression or shyness.

Body – Not unduly tall (unless ex-Guards), with a wide chest. Can go to fat quickly if not given enough to do.

Gait/Movement – Straight and true, recalling schooldays marching up and down.

Faults – Dropped H's or Estuary English are sure sign of inferior breeding.

Most Likely to Own – a Cornish fish restaurant and/or large wine cellar.

Slow-and-Steady

The Slow-and-Steady is a venerable breed, appearing wizened due to the great wrinkles of skin that he's born with. A kindly, shortsighted buffoon, he's at his most content sitting by the fireside, in the pub or on the local park bench, canine companion by his side. Known for his dogged persistence, he'll travel at a snail's pace over prodigious distances for a pint of milk and a packet of plain digestives.

Slow-and-Steadies suffer from a congenital affliction – no doubt caused by poor breeding – known as *going to beige*, which attacks the coat and trousers, which are most likely have been bright colours once. Sadly there is no cure, and the most humane course is to have him put down.

His bark should be somewhat querulous, issuing casually racist opinions over the state of British towns (especially Luton), and how much better everything was in the good old days and how, back then, youngsters had more respect.

Dog – Arthritic West Highland Terrier, King Charles Cavalier Spaniel or ancient Dachshund.

General Appearance – Short-legged, shortsighted, can run to crooked in the back. A certain amount of loose skin is desirable.

Characteristics – A slow yet determined Owner of ancient appearance, who can't help watching the world go by. Partial to a game of lawn bowls and a shake of the head in weary incomprehension. Needs television a minimum of three times a day.

Temperament – Placid, flaccid and hard to rouse. Can be affectionate with small children (loves retrieving boiled sweets from kitchen cupboards), yet timid in large crowds. Aggressive behaviour is to be seen as a fault.

Body – Short, slightly bowed legs and a bent back. A lack of hair on the top of the head but can have copious amounts at ears and nostrils. Moustaches common in both male and female, though should be discouraged.

Gait / Movement – Very slow, shuffling gait, often with use of stick or Zimmer frame. Stiff movement is an important indication and heels should drag slightly on the down-step. Susceptible to bladder problems and bogus tradesmen in later life.

Faults – Any kind of progressive opinion, tolerance of minorities or reading of newspapers other than the *Daily Mail* should be seen as a major fault. *Going to beige* discussed above.

Most Likely to Own – A privately-owned former council flat.

Tipple

A curious creature, the Tipple, when seen out of doors, always looks as though he's about to embark on a great adventure, with a heavy, waxed waterproof and stout Hunter boots, and yet never gets further than the local pub. Once safely ensconced in a warm corner with a pint and a whisky he – the female of the breed appears to be much rarer – settles down to a day of reading the racing news, dog slumped mournfully at his feet. The standard bark of the Tipple is, 'Just one more, Jack, then I'll be getting back – I only popped out to walk the dog, see.' This can be heard multiple times a day.

Dog – long suffering Border terrier.
General Appearance – Red-faced, greying, usually with a tweed cap on crown. Short and wizened, but spry when someone buys him a drink.
Characteristics – Keen for sure things at the races, always on the point of going home. Teller of bad jokes and spreader of rumours.
Temperament – Affable, gentle, of no harm to anyone. Timidity is to be expected.
Body – Short and wiry. Never gains weight.
Gait/Movement – Slow, but not a shuffler or ambler. Tends to weave about a bit when heading home.
Faults – Prone to boring conversation followed by awkward silences.
Most Likely to Own – A prodigious drinks cabinet.

Glutton

Possibly the only Owner for whom being grossly overweight is considered a breed standard, the Glutton just cannot stop eating, and neither can his dog. A creature of voracious appetite, the Glutton rarely has an empty mouth, and can often be seen outside fast food joints about to start his third breakfast. His dog lives off a continual supply of crusts and chips that fall from between the Glutton's chubby little fingers.

This breed has thrived in recent years but is exclusive to urban areas, visible on street corners in large cities and towns at all times of day and night. But the Collared Club is concerned at the growing number of instances of RSPCA call-outs to help Gluttons who've fallen over and are unable to get back up.

Due to the massive increase in Gluttons, it's possible that the breed will soon be regarded as a pest, much as the seagull is currently. While some have forecast the mandatory destruction of Gluttons at some point in the future, the specialist organization created to protect Gluttons, the Royal Astronomical Society, believes the high propensity to coronary heart disease will ensure numbers stabilize.

Dog – notoriously greedy breeds, so-called dustbins on four legs, such as Labradors and Retrievers or traditional 'street' standards like the English Bull Terrier or Staffordshire Bull Terrier (dogs with huge gaping maws catch food more easily and therefore fare better with a Glutton).

General Appearance – Just thin enough to be able to get through the doorways of takeaways and as a result cumbersome and slow. Elasticated waists and baseball caps mandatory. Heavy jewellery required in males and scrunchies in females.

Characteristics – Reliable; can work out a route that will satisfy stomach and keep to it. Unintelligible language due to mouths stuffed with grub. Lifespan roughly half of most breeds.

Temperament – Very affable unless food is withheld. Unsociable with other Owners, entirely focused on eating.

Body – Festive, with many folds for hiding emergency rations. Huge paws designed for gripping XL drinks cups.

Gait/Movement – A form of snail's-pace, a relentless waddle accompanied by short, wheezing breaths and profuse sweating.

Faults – Anything under 65 kgs in a junior or 120 kgs in an adult is seen as a serious fault.

Most Likely to Own – Males: private hire taxi cab; females – double pram or buggy (by age 15).

Mountain Hound

The Mountain Hound originated in the Italian Alps, but has become one of the most quintessentially British of Owners, as it combines a love of the outdoors with the desire to transfer weight to another's shoulders. Though slavery has been illegal since 1833, the relationship between Mountain Hound and her dog certainly has similarities. The canine is fitted with a harness, to which the Mountain Hound attaches all kinds of hiking accessories and belongings, to better free her up for steep climbs, chatting to males of the species and opportunities for selfies.

The average Mountain Hound will be sleek and muscular, though with more definition to the legs than the underworked upper body. This enables her to cover great distances at a considerable speed, the poor dog gamely trying to keep the pace. A clean breed, of a jolly temperament (as long as her dog keeps up!), She's most at home on the hilly uplands where all cares are carried by her pet.

Dog – Blindly loyal breeds such as the Collie or German Shepherd. Bernese Mountain Dogs, Newfoundlands and St Bernards also favoured for brute strength and docile temperament.

General Appearance – Well-built legs, broad thighs, but weak, narrow shoulders and upper back. However, overall, a wholesome and strong appearance.

Characteristics – Noble, with the appearance of strength and speed. Not a care in the world for the welfare of her dog.

Temperament – Always keen on having a joke, at her most cheerful when cresting a rise or reaching a summit. Prone to scolding a tardy canine.

Body – Handsome, muzzle (the males well-bearded) should carry a ruddy glow. Expensive outdoor clothing common, as are wrap-around sunglasses and a GPS. Females of the species often seen with purely decorative walking poles.

Gait/Movement – Powerful strides, able to set a furious pace, even when going near-vertical.

Faults – Any form of backpack or rucksack should be docked while the Mountain Hound is still a junior.

Most Likely to Own – An unfeasibly large Audi or Porsche 4x4.

Nat

There are three sub-breeds of Nat, with very distinct territories that closely correspond to our idea of nationhood. However, as they are all very similar, the Collared Club has decided that, as much as they would like to be kept apart, it's better to bring them together in one classification. But this comes with its own problems as anyone who has been to a Nat Show knows.

The English Nat, or as he's sometimes known, the UKIP Pointer, is an Owner with spectacularly large jowls, and is very keen on the baser things in life; beer, smoking, farting and isolationism. The sight of a European flag can cause high anxiety in the breed, including frothing at the mouth, until he can find a quiet beer garden to settle down in. There he'll while away the afternoon, telling xenophobic jokes before returning home clutching a good old English curry. If in doubt as to the variety of Nat you have spotted, listen out for his bark. If it's, 'This is political correctness gone mad!' then he's without doubt a UKIP Pointer. A delightfully ugly Owner with a pugilistic expression, he's got a reputation for tenacity, particularly about immigration, a subject he can bang on about for ages. The more bloody-minded a UKIP Pointer is, the better a standard bearer he'll be for his breed.

The Welsh Nat, or Daffy, is a rarer creature, constrained to the valleys and mountain tops of Wales. Once the prey of the UKIP Pointer (who has cannibalistic/imperialistic tendencies) he is a quiet animal for the most part, though one can hear him singing mournful songs to others of the breed across vast distances. His lungs are particularly powerful to give him the stamina to work steep mountain sheep farms so typical of his habitat. His bark is guttural, devoid of vowels, and he's never happier than when burning down a holiday cottage or two.

The Scottish Nat, or Jacobite, is a popular breed that was until recently confined to the Highlands, though is now found across Scotland in vast numbers due to a reintroduction programme that was surprisingly successful, despite a right-wing press. His public image is one of a troublemaker, but to family and friends he's cheerful and incredibly loyal. He's got a strange love of oil, and, over a whisky or six, will happily slip into a reverie for hours, dreaming that one day he'll own his own rig. Happy to curl up in an armchair, the Jacobite will become roused at the slightest provocation (for example, an attack on his legislative powers or language).

Dog – English Nat: Bulldog, Bull Terrier, Pointer, any dog with the word 'English' in its name; Welsh Nat: Corgi; Scottish Nat: Scottish/West Highland/Cairn or Skye Terrier or annoying Jack Russell.

General Appearance – Stocky, short-legged, shortsighted (inability to see other points of view); English Nat usually hairless on top with a paunch in the midriff (due to his love of Old Peculiar); Welsh Nat has large paws specifically bred for handling a rugby ball; Scot Nat has excessive amounts of wiry red hair.

Characteristics – Loyal (to his cause). Works most effectively in packs. The English Nat is prone to unforced errors when on show.

Temperament – Aggressive, protective. Prone to much whining. A reputation for not understanding the command 'No'. The highly aggressive CyberNat sub-breed has been banned through recent Dangerous Dog Owner legislation.

Body – A variety of sizes but usually, although not exclusively, in paler shades. Long muzzle to look down on others with.

Gait/Movement – Rhythmic and repetitious. Swift and deadly when attacking.

Faults – UKIP Pointer particularly susceptible to foot in mouth disease. A Nat without a grievance is to be avoided.

Most Likely to Own – English Nat: a rolled up copy of the Sun; Welsh Nat: a life-sized cut-out of Michael Sheen or Kathryn Zeta-Jones; Scottish Nat: golf clubs, bagpipes and/or a blacklist of all the No voters in his street.

Manor Born

An aristocrat amongst Owners with her bearing, demeanor and proudly carried head. Temperamentally not a breed for the masses as she can be sensitive, aloof and unsociable with more common types. To those she loves she is faithful and has an undeniable courage (particularly when dealing with trespassers or hoodies). A narrow skull and Roman muzzle gives the Manor Born a unique refinement.

The Manor Born is a pastoral in origin, but will now be found in country and suburb, where she is an incorrigible organiser, dominating parish councils, village fete committees and the local book group. It's not that she's bossy – though after a sherry or two she can become strident – but that she has a natural instinct for herding 'sheep', the result of Roedean or Cheltenham training techniques.

Though highly strung and a regular at church come Easter, Harvest or Christmas, the Manor Born is highly sexed. Behind the chintz curtains of home is a no-holds-barred world of experimentation. Males of the species invariably look careworn, if not exhausted.

Dog – Must convey 'country': ubiquitous Labrador (black or chocolate only), Border Terrier for the less affluent of the breed. Nothing that might suggest trade, such as a Collie. Occasionally something regal like a King Charles Cavalier Spaniel.

General Appearance – Well-balanced, graceful, aristocratic, dignified and elegant. Goes tweedy in old age.

Characteristics – Growls when other breeds don't approach from the rear.

Temperament – Sensitive, dominant. Becomes highly anxious in the presence of socialists. Drawn to other breeds in rebellious youth but soon realizes that other Manor Borns, or at worst a Red Trouser, are the only suitable mates.

Body – Cashmere coat in pastels (develops a thick green/brown gilet in winter). Built for speed and grace. Fringe held back from eyes by single black 'Alice band'.

Gait/Movement – A gentle sway of the hips, the Manor Born does not so much walk as glide across a room, even in heels carrying a gin.

Faults – Timidity is seen as a serious fault. Empathy with the lower orders also not to be tolerated.

Most Likely to Own – an Aga and the complete works of Jilly Cooper.

Neighbourhood Watch

Without direct aggression, the Neighbourhood Watch greets all he meets with suspicion, sniffing them intensively for several minutes before relaxing. If meeting someone for the first time, he will assume ulterior motive and nefarious purpose. This quality alone makes the breed ideal for domestic and even low-level commercial security.

In his natural environment, the cul-de-sac, he won't say much but will keep you under close observation, walking past you with his dog several times as you travel through his territory. A tracker of great quality, he has the uncanny ability to appear moments after any break-in, immediately 'pointing' at how the culprit gained entrance. Other breed characteristics include glaring at homeowners for leaving bathroom windows open ("…might as well send out a bloody invitation") or for not having house alarms, CCTV, searchlights, thermal imaging or gun emplacements.

Shakes his large head repeatedly behind the backs of policemen.

Dog – Beagle or Basset Hound. Or sometimes a toy breed such as Bichon Frisé or Yorkshire Terrier due to their incessant yappy barking at the slightest sound outside.

General Appearance – Utilitarian, never flashy, with gimlet eyes that miss nothing (usually looking for unlocked garden sheds or build-ups of junk mail). Like the Slow-and-Steady, prone to *going to beige* in old age.

Characteristics – Rabidly territorial. Highly attentive, alert, resilient and tireless when looking for hoodies. Hackles rise at young people having a good time.

Temperament – Courageous to the point of stupidity, naturally suspicious, quick to leap to (often wrong) conclusions. Tendency towards smugness and schadenfreude.

Body – Lean, twitchy, keeps in good shape to better run down hooligans and opportunist petty criminals.

Gait/Movement – A forced nonchalance.

Faults – Any departure from 'hang-em and flog-em' or 'in the old days you could leave your back door open…' pub landlord-style opinions to be seen as a serious fault.

Most Likely to Own – A pair of twitching curtains and powerful binoculars

Urban Farmer

A metropolitan owner with pastoral pretentions, the Urban Farmer is a delightful mimic. Easily spotted in city parks, particularly in newly-gentrified areas, he loves to masquerade as a more practical Owner. Males and females have beautifully pristine waterproof coats or green fleece gilets over Jermyn Street shirts. Hind legs will be sporting Hunter wellingtons (black only). Tweed caps on the crown are also excellent identifiers. His canine companion is invariably of the kind you'd expect to see herding cattle across the Serengeti rather than eyeing up squirrels in Hyde Park.

The Urban Farmer hates the rain and loves nothing more than to curl up in his favourite bistro with a Macchiato and copy of the Financial Times Weekend edition. Prone to excessive barking in crowds about 'next month's grouse shooting' or 'a wonderful smallholding in Sussex' when everyone knows he's never been outside the M25.

Dog – Springer Spaniel, Rhodesian Ridgeback, Hungarian Vizsla or Czechoslovakian Wolfdog. The more impractical the breed for city living the better. Huskies favoured 10-15 years ago until they became popular with Essex bodybuilders.

General Appearance – Handsome, active Owner, with weak or nonexistent chin.

Characteristics – Dressed for birthing cows, even if just popping to Covent Garden or Notting Hill. Gets agitated if more than five minutes' walk from a Waitrose.

Temperament – Extremely jolly if all creature comforts are at hand. Particularly fond of Michelin stars. Prone to panic north of Potters Bar.

Body – Thin, head covered in tweed or Australian wide-brimmed bush hat. Pigeon-chested.

Gait/Movement – Slow, laboured. Tends to slip on anything green. Any displays of courage undesirable.

Faults – Males congenitally prone to being born without balls.

Most Likely to Own – a Porsche Cayenne 4x4.

Helping Hand

The Helping Hand is a wonder of the species, where the symbiosis between Owner and pet is so great that all responsibility for one or more senses is handed to the dog.

Initially believed to be the result of extreme indolence, it has recently been discovered that the Helping Hand is in fact deficient in the relevant sense and delegates this function to his canine. Though there are records of similar partnerships going back centuries, the Helping Hand was not classified by the Collared Club as a breed proper until the early 20th century.

The Helping Hand will give over control of sight, smell or hearing to its dog without loss of agency. The longstanding belief that most Owner breeds also hand over urination and defecation to their pooches has recently been debunked. As payment for its services, the Helping Hand's pet is given exclusive permission to enter shops and restaurants, or go to the theatre and cinema, making it the envy of dogs everywhere.

Spotters should be aware that Helping Hands and their pets are highly active. Should you spot a comatose Labrador sporting a glazed expression and with a small slot in its head, particularly in shopping precincts, this is in fact a decoy, believed to be a remnant from the days when Helping Hands were hunted for their harnesses.

Dog – Labrador, German Shepherd or Golden Retriever.

General Appearance – Owner recognizable as a 'dude' due to the prevalence of Blues Brothers-style sunglasses. Raincoats common in both males and females. Unclear why the dog doesn't get shades as well.

Characteristics – An interest in sado-masochism common as evidenced by the elaborate harness the poor dog is forced to wear.

Temperament – Patient, docile (unless appearing on Radio 4's *In Touch* with a government minister where he instantly becomes rabid).

Body – Helping Hands come in all shapes and sizes.

Gait/Movement – Slow and steady, running not to be encouraged.

Faults – Owners who think they know better than their dog should not be used for breeding.

Most Likely to Own – A radio.

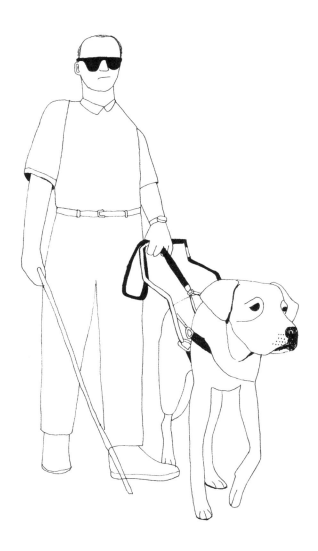

Boomerang

The Boomerang is as fat and lazy as her dog is energetic. This lack of synergy is down to the Boomerang's ingenuity in constructing or purchasing devices that can throw balls vast distances without the need for effort. She will be seen standing close to park gates, sending her dog off to fetch again and again while she checks how many likes she got for that cute photo of him she posted on Facebook.

Researchers have long been confused as to why such an unhealthy owner chooses to enter a partnership with a highly active dog. Recent genetic analysis has discovered that the Boomerang is actually the runt from a litter of Constant Trainers (see Utilitarian Group). Evidence suggests that when the all the other Constant Trainer pups follow their mother out of the nest for a quick marathon, the Boomerang stays home to carb-load on protein bars and power shakes.

Can be mistaken for a Glutton but for the presence of a throwing device and the boundless enthusiasm of the pet.

Dog – Rescued mongrel (Greyhound, Whippet, Lurcher or Collie cross).

General Appearance – Heavy build, elasticated waist.

Characteristics – Focused on food, toddlers or social media rather than her dog.

Temperament – Distracted and inattentive. Lacking in loyalty.

Body – Short legs, waist circumference 2-3 times that of the shoulders. Dainty paws evolved for manipulating smart phones.

Gait/Movement – Mostly static, painfully ponderous when actually moving, stops frequently.

Faults – Boomerangs who retrieve balls dropped by pets beyond a distance of a few feet rather than carrying several spares are regarded as inferior and unsuitable for breeding.

Most Likely to Own – A throwing stick, Frisbee, Aerobie or medieval siege catapult.

Poacher

Romance suggests that the Poacher has dainty charm, slipping through the woods at the dead of night with a ratty terrier, dosing pheasants with sleeping-raisins or popping rabbits into a hessian sack. The myth is he's a loveable rogue prone to japes and scrapes but always able to wriggle out of them with his cheeky-chappie gift of the gab, a Robin Hood of the shires. The reality is that Poacher is a feral beast – short, dirty and mean. His coat is baggy with many hidden pockets, camouflaged to blend with hedgerows and thickets.

Like the fox, Poachers are known to kill for fun, and are vicious ambush predators. They will happily live off trout, salmon, pheasant, duck, goose, deer or rabbit, and they have been known to pluck hens from coops and feast on an unwary Gamekeeper too. Few Spotters have seen an encounter between these two breeds, but they are said to be most exhilarating of cat-and-mouse battles, the Gamekeeper being larger and more powerful, while the Poacher is wily and tenacious, with a tremendous turn of speed over short distances.

Urban Poachers are becoming more common, though they prefer to leave their mongrels tied up outside to better manoeuvre the supermarket aisles that have become their forest glades. Their bodies are a different shape to their rural counterparts, leaner to slip through gaps in fences more easily, whilst retaining the many hidden pockets and compartments within their coats. The Collared Club is considering a motion to have the Urban Poacher reclassified as a breed in its own right – to be named the Shifty or High Street Shoplifter.

Dog – Poacher: Jack Russell, Border Terrier; Urban Poacher: Heinz 57 varieties mongrel.

General Appearance – A balance of stocky muscular power and strength. Built for speed and thuggery.

Characteristics – Highly adaptable to any environment. Opportunist. Silent as a Ninja when required, vicious when cornered (will bark 'Police brutality!' loudly as a distraction technique).

Temperament – When in the pub can be magnanimous, even affectionate, but when outside he becomes a voracious, single-minded predator.

Body – Chest very deep with plenty of heart room, a well-defined, broad back, with a definite Poacher's hump behind the shoulders designed for carrying or dragging twice his own weight. Whole body gives the impression of power and strength, like a coiled spring.

Gait/Movement – Shuffling and non-descript in the company of his betters but once in his preferred environment free, smooth and tireless, with minimum lift of feet, conveying the impression of ability to move with great stealth or speed when required.

Faults – General movement should never look high-stepping, short or mincing. Remorse or empathy not to be encouraged.

Most Likely to Own – A discreet lock-up with a minimum of three chest freezers.

Muscle

The Muscle is an urban Owner interested only in respect – how to gain and keep it. Known for his foolhardy levels of courage, the Muscle has a tendency to get his retaliation in first. As a result he often spends periods of time confined to kennels (also known as 'doing bird').

Often spotted by the low hang of his trouser (known as a 'hip-hop'), loose swagger and reversed baseball cap on the crown, the Muscle is one of the only Owners to still hand-forge a metal lead. He has a genuine love and compassion for his family (also known as his posse), and in his den, usually an underpass or shopping precinct, is gentleness personified. Out on the street, though, the open spaces alter the chemical balance in the Muscle's brain. As soon as he catches the scent of disrespect in the air, he will track the culprit relentlessly for hours in order to 'teach them some manners'.

Junior Muscles are partial to the lunch money of other breeds.

Dog – German Shepherd, Doberman or Rottweiler.
General Appearance – Stocky but physically well-balanced, of great strength. Tendency to walk displaying his 'packet', male jewellery and tattoos.
Characteristics – Affectionate to those considered family, but can go 'off his rocker' to prove dominance. Often seen in Chelsea or West Ham shirts.
Temperament – Bold, fearless, possibly psychotic.
Body – Muscled but with trouser legs shortened due to a bagging of skin at the groin.
Gait/Movement – Free, powerful and agile with economy of effort.
Faults – Breed prone to mentally instability and long periods of incarceration.
Most Likely to Own – A baseball bat.

Redcoat

An endangered breed owing to loss of habitat, the Redcoat is one of the few Terrierists that's a pack animal, gathering in large numbers with their hounds in order to run down hunt saboteurs. Unwilling to get their hands dirty (or indeed their feet), and by nature lazy in the extreme, they have not just formed a partnership with dogs (commonly Foxhounds or Beagles) to do their dirty work, but also with horses, in order to carry their fat arses over fences and hedges.

Bustling and full of enthusiasm, their barks of 'Tally Ho', 'What *fun*!' and 'Townies just don't get it, do they?' can be heard on bright, frosty mornings as they congregate to hunt and mate. Named because of their distinctive short russet coats with black felt markings at the collar, the common expression that Redcoats 'have a bulging wallet' usually refers to the distinctive protrusion in the tight white trousers of the males. The fact that their impressive jet-black sable helmets resemble those of constables is said to be the principle reason why they see themselves as above the law.

The Redcoat's status as endangered goes contrary to his reputation as being highly sexed, referred to by some Spotters as 'possessing the hunting horn'. However, it's the Collared Club's opinion that this species will not last the century, outside a few captive populations in Museums of Rural Life and the occasional Countryside Alliance march.

Dogs – Scent hounds such as the Foxhound or Beagle and traditionally also sight hounds such as the Greyhound or Lurcher

General Appearance – Oozes breeding (though the lack of numbers has made inbreeding prevalent, with unfortunate consequences – for examples Google 'the Bullingdon Club' or 'Tory front bench'). Conveys the impression of great superiority.

Characteristics – An Owner whose essential function is to hunt out privilege and entitlement by following a scent. Jolly and single-minded. Froths at the mouth when a fox is sighted.

Temperament – Amiable out of saddle, bloodthirsty in it. Occasionally foolhardy. Good-natured amongst its own breed but supercilious amongst Owners he deems inferior. Highly aggressive in the presence of animal rights activists.

Body – Straight-backed, large posterior with weak, bow-shaped legs due to riding everywhere. Patrician features, ruddy cheeks.

Gait / Movement – Galloping, trotting or tumbling.

Faults – Any compassion for non-domesticated species seen as a major fault. State education also highly undesirable.

Most Likely to Own – 10,000 acres in Wiltshire.

Warehouse Warrior

A nocturnal breed with a strong sense of justice, the Warehouse Warrior (or ROD: Retired On Duty) is to be found on the vast, silent industrial estates of the UK after sunset, where he hunts vandals, thieves and courting couples with his hound and heavy rubber torch. If kept in good condition a Warehouse Warrior will be alert, agile and an excellent tracker. For this reason many warehouse owners provide a warm kennel where a Warrior can read a tabloid, check delivery drivers and observe multiple CCTV monitors, all while listening to a football phone-in on the radio.

Requires huge amounts of sleep and must read at least two trashy crime thrillers a week, preferably with feet elevated on a desk of some sort. Blue serge uniform with pseudo-military peaked cap vital in fostering a misplaced sense of authority despite being on a below minimum wage zero-hours contract. The larger the epaulettes and bunch of keys the better the performance. The Warrior is a close relative of the Neighbourhood Watch but a distinct breed in his own right.

Must be kept to a strict diet of doughnuts, pizza and takeaway Chinese. If denied junk food the Warehouse Warrior becomes resentful and can develop a taste for corruption, quickly reaching the point where he'd sell his grandmother for a backhander and revenge on his employers.

Dog – German Shepherd or Doberman due to their military connotations.

General Appearance – From a distance appears compact and tough, capable of speed. In reality, most are slow, cumbersome and lacking in stamina.

Characteristics – Principally works on the element of surprise in catching his quarry, usually because he's bunking off for a cigarette and accidently stumbles upon a robbery or dogging session.

Temperament – Alert and suspicious. Shyness and lethargy is undesirable but likely.

Body – When fit he's naturally trim, straight-backed and always on the move. Early signs of decline include a barrel chest covered in biscuit crumbs.

Gait/Movement – Elastic, should be able to move from a walk to full-tilt run shouting 'Oi! You...' in a couple of seconds.

Faults – Any desire to while away the hours writing a novel renders the Warehouse Warrior wholly ineffective.

Most Likely to Own – A clip-on polyester tie.

Antisocial Animal

This is a breed with a mean streak running through her soul. The Antisocial Animal takes the guise of a good natured human being; light-hearted, sweet-tempered and fun to be around. Whilst distracting her quarry with idle chit-chat, the Antisocial Animal's pet is pissing on the doormat, having dug a large hole in the herbaceous border and will have left a huge shit on the front path. When challenged as to whom the miscreant pet belongs, the Antisocial Animal feigns outrage that it might be hers, although once inside her own home reverts to fits of laughter, taking great pleasure in the chaos her pooch has caused.

The Antisocial Animal is an excellent trainer, taking months to hone her dog's skills. In rural locations large lumbering beasts are preferred, bred to destroy sandcastles, disrupt picnics, worry sheep and leave giant dumps on narrow country paths. The urban Animal is drawn to small, stealthy dogs who will lift their leg on your trousers or Jimmy Choos before you've noticed. Public sniffing of crotches also a specialty.

Dog – Country: English Mastiff, Great Dane, Irish Wolfhound. Town: Jack Russell, Shih Tzu, Lhasa Apso, Tibetan or Yorkshire Terrier, Bichon Frisé – in other words something that looks innocuous but can be deadly.

General Appearance – Unremarkable, easy to mistake for any other breed of Owner.

Characteristics – Grudge-holding deviousness and an insatiable desire for revenge over some imaginary slight.

Temperament – Outwardly lively and vivacious, the Antisocial Animal is in fact cynical and heartless.

Body – Plump, blousy, maternal but with an icy glint.

Gait/Movement – Innocently fluid.

Faults – Any ability to take responsibility or demonstrate empathy undesirable.

Most Likely to Own – A voodoo doll.

Shagger

The Shagger is the only breed whose name doesn't refer to the Owner but his dog. The Owner is invariably nondescript, often celibate and occasionally even asexual, usually appearing a pleasant individual who enjoys meeting strangers (as it is hard for him to make friends).

Attempts to widen his social circle beyond his mother are continually thwarted by having, as his constant companion, a tiny, randy fur-ball for whom every object is demanding to be humped with the abandon of impending annihilation by a giant asteroid.

Due to the affable but engrossed nature of the Shagger's conversation, those who're having their leg, shoe or even arm taken advantage of find it very hard to complain or even mention what's occurring, especially when such an interest is being shown in that holiday they took to Corfu four years previously. The skill of the Owner is to appear completely oblivious to the actions of his dog. The reality is that due to the lack of love and affection in his own life he lives vicariously through his sex-mad pet.

Dog – small, hyperactive breeds such as Chihuahua, Papillon, Bichon Frisé, Maltese and Yorkshire Terrier.

General Appearance – The Owner looks unremarkable and is difficult to distinguish from other breeds besides a mad glint in the eye of his pet. Sometimes seen in socks and sandals (the Owner not the pet).

Characteristics – A predator designed to blend into his surroundings, uses surprise and the goodwill of others to launch sustained attacks.

Temperament – Appears chatty, attentive, curious. In reality, lonely and manipulative.

Body – Coat from Debenhams own label, or Primark, in tan, magnolia or beige. Jeans ironed with a crease in a Corby Trouser Press.

Gait/Movement – Ambling with a hint of purposelessness.

Faults – Any outward signs of gratification will seriously hamper the Shagger's ability to function and may result in a jail term.

Most Likely to Own – A hidden camera.

Parson's Nose

With a glossy black coat and distinctive flash of white under the chin, the Parson's Nose is a noble if somewhat lugubrious breed. Instantly recognisable for his tendency to look to the heavens, clasping his paws together, at the first sign of trouble.

Named in respect to his extraordinary olfactory skills, the Parson's Nose is prized for his ability to sniff out emotional problems in others, tenacious rooting around in the hinterland of their personal lives until he discovers the cause. He also loves the sound of his own bark, a long, low drone that can go on and on for hours at a time.

The English Parson's Nose only mates to procreate, and never enjoys it (hence why the Purple Breasted Bishop sub-breed is so rare), while the Irish Parson's Nose is celibate (or claims to be) but is famed for his love of children. The fearsome Ulster Parson's Nose is highly aggressive and is particularly adept at hunting Catholics and members of the LGBTI community.

The breed's ability to eat anything placed in front of it, particularly at weddings and funerals, should not be encouraged.

Dog – Beagle, Bloodhound, Basset Hound, German Shepherd, Miniature Pinscher, Pomeranian (all deafening regardless of size)

General Appearance – Tall and thin (where possible), bold, with a defiant carriage of head and an intelligent if supercilious expression.

Characteristics – Intelligent (often bookish), lively with a sherry in him and with a strong moral compass. Especially suited to addressing large groups in drafty spaces.

Temperament – Faithful, versatile and good tempered (except for the Ulster which is extremely grumpy).

Body – Sloping shoulders, may stoop slightly, increasing with age. Wide chest, allowing ample capacity for development of a large heart and lungs.

Gait/Movement – This should be free and flowing, with a long stride driven by the hindquarters. Feet slightly splayed, often flat.

Faults – Signs of independent thinking not to be encouraged.

Most Likely to Own – Often has an impressive collection of skeletons in his closet.

Muck Spreader

An ancient breed, the name Muck Spreader is a misnomer in the modern age. Even as little as thirty years ago it was common to see this Owner, with a small bucket or trug, carrying his and other dogs' fecal matter out of the city to spread it on designated spaces called allotments. This is believed to have been some kind of religious or mating ritual.

The great irony for the Muck Spreader is that, having pioneered a behaviour that has now become widespread, namely the collection of poo in receptacles, those Muck Spreaders who don't use the now socially mandatory 'little black poo bag' but revert to their preferred bucket are often seen as mentally ill. This results in regular visits from social services and even, in extreme cases, incarceration, the main reason for the swift decline in numbers in the British Isles.

In the present day the easiest way to spot a Muck Spreader is one of three ways. Firstly, due to his deeply ingrained instincts, the Muck Spreader tends to be drawn to canines that are prodigious defecators. Secondly, watch his expression as he collects poo. Whereas most other Owners' faces will invariably register disgust as the warmth of a newly deposited crap is felt through the thin plastic bag as it's picked up, the Spreader will smile with pleasure. Thirdly, watch closely as the Spreader drops the sealed poo bag in the bin. More often than not, a single tear will roll down his cheek as he feels the loss as keenly as a death in the family.

Dog – Walking biomass plants like the Great Dane, Rottweiler, Mastiff and Wiemaraner

General Appearance – Careworn, stooped, often dressed for agriculture.

Characteristics – A natural loner, principally due to the smell emanating from his pail.

Temperament – A tendency to hoarding and a bit paranoid that the men in white suits are out to get him.

Body – Short legs, stocky, strong shoulders, powerful front paws, strong lower back for bending.

Gait/Movement – Plodding, prone to stopping at regular intervals.

Faults – Poor sense of smell will seriously hamper the Muck Spreader in finding and collecting his prizes.

Most Likely to Own – Industrial strength soap.

Broken Athlete

A relative of the Constant Trainer, once thought to be the product of rampant inbreeding, though now recognized by the Club as a breed in his own right, the Broken Athlete is a slow-moving Owner, with an exclusive affinity with old racing Greyhounds.

Like the Urban Farmer, the Broken Athlete is an excellent mimic. Recognizable as closely resembling a once great sportsman; someone who excelled in his chosen field and now suffers greatly for having pushed his body to the limit again and again. This of course is a complete fabrication, and the Broken Athlete was in fact born creaking, with painful muscle spasms, early onset arthritis, and yet with the noble bearing of someone who may have been a contender, once.

You will often find him walking through urban parks, stopping to watch as joggers pass by, yearning for activity he's never taken part in. A melancholic beast, he's best left to his own devices, as his gloom is contagious.

Dog – Arthritic Greyhound, the more mournful the better.
General Appearance – Shiny coat in lurid colours, known as a 'shell suit'. Walks stiffly with little or no fluidity. Sweat on brow.
Characteristics – Remarkably little stamina. Happiest curled up on a sofa.
Temperament – A quiet dignity, tendency towards introspection.
Body – Wasted muscle on a lean frame. Chest deep, suggesting aerobic powers now vanished.
Gait/Movement – Hobbling.
Faults – When under threat, in fight or flight mode, if the Broken Athlete moves with speed it should not be bred.
Most Likely to Own – A disabled parking blue badge or mobility scooter.

Vegan

Although generally good-natured, the Vegan has an idiosyncratic, sour-faced look, much admired by advocates of the breed. This, coupled with a raised nose and low brow, gives her a distinctive, haughty expression developed over centuries of disapproving of meat-eating in all its guises.

The Vegan is cut short on the crown, the remaining fur often in gelled spikes and even shaved at one or both sides, known as a 'punky' by groomers. When at show, the muzzle and ears should be adorned with rings and piercings.

Due to private training, this is not a resilient breed, having an innate appreciation of the finer things in life. She cannot breed more than five miles from a Wholefoods or market garden collective.

Dog – Rescued mongrel with an expression of gross disappointment due to an exclusively vegetarian dog food diet.

General Appearance – Small, wiry with an intense expression. Flowing coat of Indian origin or baggy denim dungarees. Hind paws of black 'Dr Marten' shape. May display a collar tag announcing ownership by social services or community sexual health.

Characteristics – Becomes excitable when smelling a cause. Prone to a repeating bark of 'I've met Banksy, you know…'

Temperament – Generally kind and loyal but grows anxious in the company of Redcoats.

Body – Petite, but with powerful hind legs due to much cycling.

Gait/Movement – Kinetic, determined stride.

Faults – If the Vegan doesn't respond to the call 'Monbiot' then it may be worth considering putting to sleep.

Most Likely to Own – A cupboard full of mung beans and a yoga mat.

Muzzler

Instantly recognizable by the elaborate adornment of his pet with shiny metal choke chains, muzzles, chest harnesses, coquettish leather straps, studded collars and leads, the Muzzler's link to German BDSM sub-culture is immediately apparent to all who observe this fascinating nocturnal breed in his natural environment in and around the late night club scene.

The Muzzler is an urban animal with a robust, athletic physique of rippling muscle and tattoos. His threatening appearance (he usually has a lot of metal in his own face) can make him unpopular with the older generation, although he's known as a big-hearted sop and is highly submissive in the presence of other Owners and Doms.

Once in a safe, domestic environment, the Muzzler's amorous nature shines through. A demanding playmate, he's prone to jumping, licking, nibbling, biting and all manner of other highly energetic games.

Dog – Bull Terriers are a favourite, but any size or breed will do.
General Appearance – Strong and athletic, glossy black (in summer a coat of black leather trousers and Metallica t-shirt; in winter develops a thick rubber hide) and prominent forequarters. Loves displaying his long, studded tongue with a quick, flicking motion.
Characteristics – Appears intimidating but often this is to disguise a soft, high-pitched, lisping bark.
Temperament – Misbehaves because he enjoys being scolded so much.
Body – Well defined musculature, broad shoulders and powerful forelegs.
Gait / Movement – Slightly bow-legged waddle for theatrical effect.
Faults – Should canine adornment develop into full costume syndrome (e.g. dog dressed as clown, Superman etc.) then highly unsuitable for breeding.
Most Likely to Own – A large collection of vintage crocodile clips.

Constant Trainer

The Constant Trainer is a lean, mean running machine, built for speed, power and endurance. Tall and rangy, he can be stand-offish with other breeds who don't conform to his body image or fitness regime. He's highly competitive with other Trainers, especially during the rutting season, where huge numbers gather to 'run a marathon', a spectacular event, part migration, part rite of sexual conquest.

Spotters are encouraged to use hides in trees or buildings during marathons or fun runs to avoid being mistaken for a rival or simply trampled in the rush for the finish line. The real pleasure of a Constant Trainer for any Spotter is watching him run with his canine companion on a lead or tied to his waist by an elastic rope. There's a reach and strength to his stride that's poetry in motion.

But beware, he's also got a mean streak and is not above teasing a Broken Athlete mercilessly should he come across one. They've also been known to descend on shops selling powdered protein *on masse*, much in the way locusts descend on crops, cleaning out the shelves in a matter of minutes of anything overpriced or pseudo-medical.

Dog – Long-legged canines used to running long distances including the Springer Spaniel, Dalmatian, English Setter, Collie, Jack Russell (believe it or not), Weimaraner, Lurcher, Ridgeback and Husky.

General Appearance – Tall and athletic, toned on the side of skinny with zero body fat.

Characteristics – Addicted to endorphins, competitive and self-obsessed but very useful if you're fighting a battle in Greece and need to send messages back and forth.

Temperament – Single-minded and relentless.

Body – Long-legged, with little or no body fat.

Gait/Movement – Loping.

Faults – Lack of competitiveness highly disadvantageous.

Most Likely to Own – Running shoes that cost more than your car.

Farming Subsidy

This energetic breed has a deep-seated need for work. At home in pastoral environments of all kinds, from muddy fields and summer pastures to bleak, windswept hillsides, he's a natural loner. His jowls, whiskers and furrowed brow give the Farming Subsidy a somewhat taciturn disposition.

Never happier than when bounding through a bog or running up scree, he does become anxious about unseasonal weather and the late arrival of cheques from the Department for Agriculture and Rural Development. Also demonstrates great antipathy towards townies and supermarket milk aisles, both of which should be avoided to prevent unnecessary stress.

When training a Farming Subsidy he's best motivated by the regular reward of listing grievances, from overall government agricultural policy and foreign imports to the price of rural property and organic versus intensive. However, as anyone who's worked with a Farming Subsidy knows, this list is endless – 'little and often' is strongly advisable otherwise no work will get done.

The breed is characterised by lack of grace compensated by raw power. Language skills are basic, but they respond to most signals – audible or visual – invariably with grunts or the occasional long list of profanities. The West Country Farming Subsidy exists solely on cheese and cider. If left alone for long periods may try and crossbreed with sheep.

Dog – Border Collie mandatory (Jack Russell optional).

General Appearance – Well-proportioned, green or brown coat of tweed or fleece (enhanced with a thick layer of Goretex in winter) and checked underfur. Smooth outline of quality and balance, conveying endurance. Older specimens will have leathery, weather-beaten skin, many wrinkles and thick, wiry hair growing from every orifice.

Characteristics – Tenacious, hard-working but no great thinker.

Temperament – Keen, alert, responsive, if only with muttered expletives. Loves barking 'Get off my land!' at those trespassing on his territory.

Body – Athletic in appearance, though easily runs to fat if spending too much time *in tractor*, as the Romans put it.

Gait/Movement – Plodding, as if wading through mud, which they probably are.

Faults – An interest in art, wider culture or the modern world in general highly undesirable.

Most Likely to Own – Ten Landrovers in varying states of decomposition.

Hydra

A breed once thought to be mythical, the Hydra first appeared in the early nineties and has been reproducing vigorously ever since. Only seen in city parks in daylight hours, he's known for his highly promiscuous relationships with canines.

The average adult Hydra has between 6 and 12 dogs, and those who have the widest variety of shapes, sizes and breeds have greatest social status. It's believed that the Hydra gains more dogs when rutting. As two Hydras come together, if one dog is 'lost' when a lead breaks, at least two more grow in its place.

For beginners, the Hydra is recognisable as a single harassed Owner in the middle of a mass of leads and dogs, which he uses for propulsion, much like an Arctic sledder. He travels at great speed down narrow paths, scattering all in his wake. He particularly enjoys getting tangled with buggies, lampposts, benches and other Owners, this being his principal form of social interaction.

Some experts believe this crisscrossing of leads may be a form of web, those small creatures unfortunate enough to become entangled being his main source of sustenance. Some at the Collared Club reckon the Hydra is not a breed but a parasite, suggesting he's not an Owner at all but 'borrows' dogs from breeds of idle Owner glued to the sofa 'at work'. To my mind the jury's out and, till proved otherwise, I'll give him the benefit of the doubt.

Dog – That'll be dogs, not dog. Any breed, of any size or shape, the more the merrier. The Hydra isn't choosy.

General Appearance – A whirlwind of fur and lead, with an owner inside who is hard to see, but may have a short, brightly-coloured, quilted coat and some sort of peaked cap. Usually leaves a trail of discarded poo bags and treats in his wake.

Characteristics – Fast, furious, and extremely dangerous.

Temperament – Hard to tell but appears permanently flustered. Single-minded, certainly.

Body – Again very difficult to observe but from long lens photography appears short, stocky with immensely powerful shoulders and forepaws.

Gait/Movement – A blur of speed.

Faults – Two dogs does not a Hydra make.

Most Likely to Own – A dwindling redundancy package or inadequate pension.

Untrained

The Untrained is easy to spot as she is the exact reverse of the Constant Trainer. While the latter runs and runs, his pet struggling to keep up, the former is always chasing after her dog, barking commands that the pet takes great delight in ignoring. The Untrained will yell terrible profanities whilst simultaneously apologising profusely to all those fleeing in terror of her marauding pooch. Just search YouTube for 'Fenton chasing deer in Richmond Park' for a perfect video example of an Untrained in the wild.

The Untrained is unique in her complete lack of affinity with her dog. Indeed, a question mark exists over who owns whom in the relationship. Many believe the Owner is in fact the dog – the only example of complete canine dominance you'll find. Nonetheless, this makes the Untrained very agile and active, due to the running she's forced to undertake. The Untrained has Olympic levels of stamina and a vast capacity for being sorry.

If you're lucky enough to observe an Untrained in her domestic environment, you'll most likely see her curled up with her pet on the sofa, watching TV. This demonstrates there is a bond of sorts between Owner and dog. However, researchers are unsure who'll have chosen the channel.

Dog – Large, willful animals such as the Labrador, Husky or German Shepherd or intellectually challenged dogs like the Airedale or Red Setter.

General Appearance – Flustered, crimson cheeks from constant whistling, running and abject embarrassment. Wide eyed with 'sorry' always on the tip of her tongue.

Characteristics – Capable of great endurance and a fair turn of speed, though never quite enough to catch her dog!

Temperament – Never hesitant, but prone to panic and suffers from guilt. Constant, excruciating guilt.

Body – When running, lithe and supple. At rest hunched, attempting to make herself as small and unobtrusive as possible.

Gait/Movement – Moves from all-out sprint to stumbling hesitancy as each canine atrocity is committed.

Faults – Any signs of not giving a shit undesirable in this breed. Easy embarrassment essential.

Least Likely to Own – The Dog Whisperer DVD Box Set

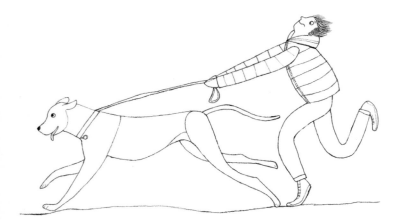

Walked

The Walked is a marvel of evolution. He defies gravity, possessing the ability to travel in a forwards direction whilst leaning at a 45 degree angle backwards. This is because his dog is at least one and half times (but preferably twice) his size.

Whether this Owner is attracted to such an impractical pooch due to a love of huge dogs or a perceived inadequacy in the trouser department remains to be seen. However the Walked has developed a highly specialised, wild-eyed, bow-legged trot as he proves incapable of resisting a primitive desire for perpetual and violent forward motion.

Understandably the Walked is reluctant to socialise with other breeds. He will often cite the care of his oversized companion as an excuse for not conversing with others but, as any Spotter will see, he is clearly aware that if he tries to stop he'll lose balance and be dragged face down through the streets for at least a mile.

Dog – Great Dane, Mastiff, Rottweiler, Husky, Malamut, Newfoundland, Bernese Mountain Dog, Black Russian Terrier.
General Appearance – Squat, large hind paws with rubber soles for traction.
Characteristics – Grimacing as he tries to exert some kind of discipline over his Leviathan, desperate to appear in control when he clearly isn't.
Temperament – Wants to enjoy the status of a prestige canine but can't. Driven by fear and the survival instinct.
Body – Powerful, but not quite powerful enough.
Gait/Movement – Stuttering, jerky, with straining muscles.
Faults – Any Owner with a dog less than one and a half times its size.
Most Likely to Own – Poo bags the size of elephant condoms.

Sob Story

The Sob Story is recognisable as an almost exclusively urban breed. Split into three sub-breeds, you'll find the indigenous Hard Times, the Scrounger and the exotic Continental on British high streets in varying numbers.

The Hard Times is the most recognizable, poorly fed with its thin coat of cagoule, its best known for being Kennel-less. The Hard Times Sob Story has a dog that, while medium to large, is selected for its mournful, pleading expression. This is because everyone knows that the British feel far greater empathy for animals than humans.

For varying reasons, from addiction and mental health problems to marital breakdown, joblessness and the shrinking of the welfare state, the Hard Times becomes unable to fend for itself and must rely on support from passers-by. This is a fragile, vulnerable breed and should be helped wherever possible to prevent extinction.

The Scrounger is a semi-mythical interloper, a mimic, who pretends to be a Hard Times Sob Story but is in fact 'living the high life on benefits'. Beloved of readers of the tabloid press and television documentary makers, who appear utterly obsessed with it, the Scrounger and his cur are adept at extracting money through false advertising. However there's little evidence to suggest that the Scrounger actually exists. After all, why would anyone choose to sit on the street in the rain all day, begging, if they didn't have to?

The Continental Sob Story or Economic Migrant, a breed of Owner of Romanian descent, is much rarer than many make out. Its existence and nomadic patterns vex politicians and newspaper editors who believe that *Daily Mail* readers must be pandered to at every opportunity. Despite its jolly demeanor, flat cap or headscarf and ability to play musical instruments badly, it's treated with hostility and even violence by wide sections of society.

Dog – A mongrel, preferably with a skin problem such as scabies or mange.

General Appearance – Hard Times looks cold, malnourished and a stranger to a bar of soap. His coat is dirty and matted. The Scrounger looks much the same but, come sunset, changes into elegant robes before descending, with his pooch, into a Jacuzzi in the middle of his bedsit – or so they say. The Continental is small, leathery and dances in circles to the music from the strange fiddle with a trumpet attachment that he plays.

Characteristics – Quiet, sedentary breed, mostly urban but occasionally found in the country under hedges.

Temperament – Timid with a quiet, sad bark of 'Spare some change?'.

Body – Skinny, ribs visible, shivers uncontrollably when not in brilliant sunshine.

Gait / Movement – Very rare to see a Sob Story moving at all.

Faults – Smiling or laughter is not to be tolerated in this breed.

Most Likely to Own – Nothing.

Fraidy

A classic teacup breed (its teacup rattles at the slightest sound), everyone and everything is a threat to the Fraidy and her dog, and she will protect it to the last. A compact breed of Owner, twitchy and hyper-sensitive to peripheral movement at its smallest and most innocuous, she is to her dog as a mother hen is to her chicks, shielding her canine from all the dangers of the world.

Whether it be leaves blowing ominously, a bird that's looking at them funny or the wholly unpredictable behavior of that mobster of municipal open spaces, the squirrel, each sends the Fraidy and her pup scuttling home. And heaven forbid it starts raining…

As a direct result, the Fraidy's dog tends to look bored and weak – the result of a complete absence of proper exercise. Occasionally you might spot a pair that's overweight, though the all-pervading threat of heart disease is usually enough ensure the Fraidy keeps her pet on a strictly regimented diet. In some cases the Fraidy's overprotective nature creates a dog that, when the owner is asleep, will slip out of the house, go joy-riding, get into fights and score doggy heroin down the Rescue Centre.

Dog – Small dogs are preferred by this breed, as they are much easier to pick up when fleeing from other Owners: Chihuahua, Yorkshire Terrier, Papillon, Teacup Poodle, Pug, French Bulldog, Boston Terrier, Lhasa Apso, Shih Tzu, King Charles Cavalier Spaniel, Bichon Frisé etc.

General Appearance – Small with tiny legs and huge fear-filled eyes.

Characteristics – Only emerges from its kennel for brief periods. Dissolves in the rain.

Temperament – Timid in the extreme but with a fierce maternal instinct.

Body – Small, compact, built for quick darting movements. Large front paws for scooping up her pet.

Gait/Movement – Staccato, hesitant, but extreme fast over short distances.

Faults – A tan of any kind suggests she's been out in sunlight and therefore is a poor example of the breed.

Most Likely to Own – A bullet proof VW Polo.

Melancollie

The Melancollie is a lone ranger, shunned by all other breeds of Owner. Usually spotted sitting on park benches or on seaside promenades, alone in the rain, this depressed animal feeds through consuming the happy thoughts of others, before periodically excreting stools of highly concentrated misery. These pellets of pure despair are much sought-after for recycling in soap operas and in the scripts of hard-hitting Channel 4 documentaries.

If you spot a Melancollie, with his faithful companion waiting patiently at his feet as he stares into space, don't be tempted to approach. Like a horse tick, he'll fix onto you, slowly sucking you of any joy with tales of medical misdiagnosis, failed marriages, unhappy childhoods and redundancy.

The Melancollie isn't found exclusively out-of-doors. In the winter he hibernates in the corner of your local pub. You'll spot him sitting in silence, ignored by the other customers and staff, nursing a single pint of stout for hours, as his dog licks the crumbs from the sticky carpet.

Dog – Small, patient, unobtrusive breeds such as a Lurcher cross.
General Appearance – Plainly or even shabbily dressed, two day grey stubble.
Characteristics – A cloud of gloom hangs over the head of the Melancollie.
Temperament – Despondent but craves an audience.
Body – Overweight but not morbidly so.
Gait/Movement – Entirely dormant. If you're lucky enough to see one at anything other than rest then mostly likely he'll be shuffling along slowly, staring at the ground as he walks.
Faults – A liking for sitcoms precludes the Melancollie from showing.
Most Likely to Own – a *The Best of Leonard Cohen* CD or a toy Eeyore.

Wag

The Wag is one of the most iconic and glamorous categories of Dog Owner. Its name is nothing to do with the vigorous tail action of its canine companion but dates back to the origins of the breed. In the late nineteenth century it was championed by the mustachioed, Brylcremed, baggy shorts wearing exponents of the then new sport of association football. Great rivalry existed between the players of leading teams such as Preston North End, Accrington Stanley and Notts County, to see who could possess the most elegant, well-groomed Wag in the league.

The breed standard includes long legs, delicate features and voluminous fur (in 'bottle blonde' or 'gypsy black') on the crown. The Wag is famous for her imperious expression with which she looks at – and through – any stranger.

The Wag's sole concern is grooming, and she will spend hours at the parlour making sure she achieves 'Loaded' standard, the classification by which Wags are judged in competition (although the rival 'Nuts' and 'Zoo' scales have challenged this in recent years). She will have a team of experts working on all aspects of her presentation, seeking to achieve the Sunny Delight orange coat for which the breed is famous.

The Wag was originally bred for hunting, and is always on the lookout for a tasty catch to live off. Her method of killing is regarded by many as distasteful, cornering her quarry in a nightclub or Prada outlet before bleeding him dry over months or even years. As a result, she needs very little in the way of additional sustenance, existing on no more than one bag of salad and carton of almond milk a week.

Dog – Chihuahua, Bichon Frisé, Pug, French Bulldog or Papillon. Must fit in a Chanel handbag.

General Appearance – Head held proudly. Gives the impression of power and wealth. Dignified. Simply stunning to observe in motion (walking through Harrods).

Characteristics – Bores easily. Extraordinary ability to sniff out money.

Temperament – Dignified and aloof with a fierceness when faced with a dwindling bank balance.

Body – Slim and toned. Hipbones rather prominent as a result. An unnatural depth of chest.

Gait/Movement – Languid, never needing to move quickly for anyone (unless at aerobics class or nose down, ranging through an exclusive department store).

Faults – Any example that hasn't be modified cosmetically in some way should be regarded as inferior.

Most Likely to Own – A mirror or twelve, and her own perfume brand.

Long Leadtime

The curse of the urban jungle, this is a breed universally despised. She's attached to her (usually small, snuffling) dog by an extendable chord of extraordinary proportions. While the Long Leadtime stands and chats to a friend in the park or bellows into her mobile telephone on a street corner, the extendable lead allows said pooch to roam as far and wide as it pleases. As the dog inevitably wraps itself around a tree or lamppost, the principle purpose of the Leadtime's behaviour seems to be to trip up old people and castrate passing cyclists.

The Owner spends much of her time untangling her Dog and as a result has evolved long, thin paws with sharp claws for the purpose. One theory is that the Long Leadtime's leash was originally a skipping rope and she intended to teach her pup to skip. However, as everyone knows dogs are shit at skipping. Another thesis proposes that the Long Leadtime is the female equivalent of the Muzzler and, when she's bored, the lead doubles up as a bullwhip.

Note: some new research suggests that the Long Leadtime is a puppy stage of the Hydra, though this has yet to be verified and, as such, she retains her own classification.

Dog – Pug, Shih Tzu, Tibetan Terrier, King Charles Cavalier Spaniel, Boston Terrier, Jack Russell.

General Appearance – Small and active, with a fine head of fur. Generally very handsome and often expensively dressed.

Characteristics – Fabulous at ignoring her dog to the point that, from a distance, it's impossible to tell if they are actually together or not.

Temperament – Focused on anything other than her pet until she has to unpick the giant knot created.

Body – Slim, able to move quickly when she chooses with perfect balance at all times.

Gait/Movement – Likes travelling at right angles or in the opposite direction to her dog.

Faults – The lead or chord should extend to at least three metres for an Owner in show condition. If the dog can skip, even better.

Most Likely to Own – Baden Powell's *Knots and How to Untie Them* or *The Big Book of Kinbaku*.

Mobile Home

The Mobile Home is a sad breed where the power dynamic between Owner and dog is unbalanced (with the pet calling all the shots), similar to, but not as extreme as, the Untrained. For the beginner, this is identifiable through the way the dog 'drives' the human, in much the same way as a fat man drives a truck. Such is the intellectual capacity of the pooch, and the ability of the Owner limited, the Mobile Home's dog will force her to carry it in some sort of ridiculous bag or harness, telling her where to go and what to do.

Such is the strength of the dog's control that the Owner's faculties become seriously impaired, leaving her a near husk, only capable of inanities, and are easily distracted by shiny, sparkly things.

There has long been a debate within the Collared Club that an end should be put to this pathetic breed with a worldwide sterilisation order, but it has been answered with a well-crafted defence. It argues for maintaining the ecosystem of Owners, as who knows what the effects of such a program might be on the wider species. At heart there's a fear that dogs capable of manipulating a Mobile Home so successfully might find a way to infect humanity if their preferred host was no longer around.

Dog – Chihuahua, Maltese, Pug, Yorkshire Terrier.

General Appearance – Small, dainty, woefully stupid.

Characteristics – Easily trained if offered the right amounts of bling.

Temperament – Always happy and smiling, if never entirely sure what is going on. Permanently quizzical.

Body – Thin, due to the dog's lack of interest in the Owner's needs. Head large and doll-like.

Gait/Movement – A slow, calm, graceful stride. The Mobile Home never rushes in case its pet gets travelsick.

Faults – Literacy undesirable.

Most Likely to Own – Gucci, Versace et al.

In-Fashion

Also known as the Hoxton Hipster, this is a breed utterly ignorant of the fact it's mocked by all others. As with his taste in clothes and music, the In-Fashion chooses his dog by what he feels is fashionable, quirky or obscurely exotic at any particular time and not for any emotional reason.

You'll see him only in the trendiest urban areas, listening to experimental noise music in his bright yellow coat, bobble hat and skinny jeans, arguing with others of the breed over where the best Frappuccino might be found and extolling the virtues of making his own sausages. For the beginner, the In-Fashion is easily spotted by his impressive, if ridiculous, facial hair, which is a substitute for having a personality.

The In-Fashion tries to out-do others by breeding evermore heinously cool hybrid dogs from the now tiresome mass market (and thereby deeply undesirable) cockerpoo and jackahuahua to the afadoor or even the poor old cheagle.

Luckily, he doesn't often stray beyond his usual habitat other than participating in occasional mass excursions to the countryside on his fixed-gear bicycle – a mating migration that sadly means the continuation of the breed.

Dog – Any crossbreed that involves a stupid name, just don't call it a mongrel.

General Appearance – Huge amounts of facial hair, checked coat often recycled from other breeds.

Characteristics – Appearance over substance every time.

Temperament – Prone to whining about how they were into some band before they were famous.

Body – Skinny, angular, groomed in extreme, almost farcical, ways.

Gait/Movement – Normally easy and free-flowing unless carrying large amounts of vinyl.

Faults – Self-awareness not advisable.

Most Likely to Own – A reel-to-reel tape recorder, because like the In-Fashion it's cool but useless.

Flamboyant Friends

The Flamboyant Friends is a unique breed involving two Owners and one dog in a bizarre *ménage a trois*. Two males enter into a civil partnership with a pet, the contract for which states that in return for huge amounts of pampering and the bestowing of many gifts of great value, the dog must be willing to be dressed up at any time without warning.

The costumes involved range from elegant, expensive, imported Japanese dog jackets and bootees to full celebrity and superhero outfits. The tie-dying of fur in hilariously lurid colours is also mandatory.

A Flamboyant Friends' social life usually involves meeting up with other Flamboyant Friends (with their own pooches dressed as Marilyn, Woody from Toy Story or a Sad Clown). They talk loudly and demonstratively but behind each other's back are very bitchy about the others' pet.

Dog – Toy breeds preferred but anything that looks a scream in a wig and sunglasses.

General Appearance – Varies greatly between sub-breeds; Twinky, Bear, Cub, Jock and Stud.

Characteristics – Loud, high-pitched (occasionally shrill) bark. Kind, loving and overly generous to their canine. Must have the latest canine adornment or accessory on the market.

Temperament – Prone to public displays of affection with their pooch every 30 seconds.

Body – Entirely depends on the sub-breed (see above), ranges from pubescent skinniness to big 'n' cuddly.

Gait/Movement – Delightfully light lift of the paws, energetic and enthusiastic with a comic swivel of the hips.

Faults – Shyness is a major fault in this breed (unless faux coquettishness).

Most Likely to Own – *Vagazzle Your Dog in Three Easy Steps.*

White Russian

Previously rare in the UK (apart from a brief flurry of interest in the breed after 1917), the White Russian has been imported in far greater numbers in recent years after a major breeding programme in its native land instigated by the Yeltsin Club. She's most recognisable for her thick, opulent, bullet-proof coat and her predilection for purchasing cavernous kennels she never sets foot in.

Predominantly found in London's most expensive boroughs (although breeding pairs have been seen hovering above Highland estates), she's a specimen of Owner that's accustomed to a pampered lifestyle, requiring significant upkeep, including hourly grooming. She exists exclusively on Beluga Caviar and Champagne although the liberal application of foie gras mixed with vodka is known to greatly improve the lustre of her fur.

The White Russian is a sociable breed, famous for buying friends, politicians, super yachts and much-loved high street institutions.

Dog – Any hound requiring hours of pampering to look fabulous, such as a poodle, borzoi or rough collie.
General Appearance – Elegant but with a sinister glint in her eye.
Characteristics – Affectionate and generous with her friends. Can be stubborn if challenged by foreign governments.
Temperament – Loves the rich and famous, highly acquisitive and prone to collecting many 'toys'. Pathological fear of umbrellas.
Body – Extraordinary buying power from a standing start.
Gait/Movement – Famous for her smooth acceleration, also known as the 'Rolls Royce' movement.
Faults – Susceptible to rampant Capitalism.
Most Likely to Own – Everything and everyone.

Non-Dom

The Non-Dom is a mythical beast that has not been sighted for hundreds of years, though it's my firm belief he does exist. The biggest clue to his presence is his dog – usually a large, shaggy breed, extremely well-fed – which can be spotted gamboling on the beaches of seaside towns that happen to be hosting Tory or UKIP political party conferences.

While the Non-Dom will be nowhere to be seen, said canine will be the charge of some junior member of the Non-Dom's staff who, while not the Owner, will be finding the pooch impossible to control and will be responsible for clearing up copious amounts of shit left in its wake – a remarkable parallel with those unfortunate enough to work directly for the Non-Dom himself.

Tradition suggests that the Non-Dom loves to root around the fringes of politics, has a strong nose for self-interest and a penchant for influencing government policy in his favour.

Dog – Newfoundland, Bernese Mountain Dog, Irish Wolfhound, Scottish Deer Hound, Mastiff.

General Appearance – Unknown due to his rarity.

Characteristics – Brilliant at circumventing laws and tax, and stabbing former allies in the back.

Temperament – Elusive but known to be highly dominant, stubborn and determined to get his own way.

Body – Believed to be corpulent across the midriff due to a preference for very rich diets and helicopter travel.

Gait/Movement – Highly agile especially when escaping prosecution.

Faults – Philanthropy not to be encouraged.

Most Likely to Own – Belize.

Runaway

The Runaway is a hybrid, an Owner bred without a dog. He's a sad creature, a Cuckoo of the Owner kingdom, regarded as an exotic abomination by many traditionalists in the Collared Club. He can be spotted in parks and on high streets approaching groups of other Owners to ask if 'anyone has seen my dog'. This is believed to be a ruse, designed to distract an Owner before attempting to misappropriate her hound.

Not a predator as such, in the way that the Poacher, Hydra or Shagger is, I believe the Runaway is to be pitied, so bereft is he that he has lost his (non-existent) pooch.

If you know the breed is operating in your area, the best defence against a Runaway making off with your pet is to keep a reasonably life-like canine cuddly toy with you at all times. So emotionally fragile is he that if you say 'is this him?' and hand over the soft toy, most likely he'll clutch it to his bosom and then flee with a cackle.

Dog – Tragically dogless.
General Appearance – Shabby, distracted, with large watery, bloodshot eyes.
Characteristics – Irritatingly persistent. Prone to begging.
Temperament – Vulnerable but manipulative.
Body – Powerful legs for a speedy getaway.
Gait / Movement – Frantic, distracted energy.
Faults – Substitute pets such as gerbils or hamsters can seriously hamper the breed's natural instincts.
Most Likely to Own – A DVD of Disney's *The Incredible Journey*.

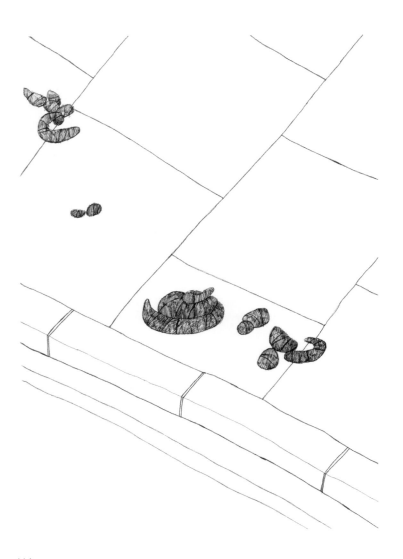

Phantom

The Phantom is as elusive as the Scottish Wildcat or Sumatran Tiger but I am sure that most members of the general public will have come across the evidence of his or her existence. That is of course their trademark tracks.

All one ever sees of the Phantom is the steaming piles of dog crap left abandoned in the middle of the pavement, day after day. No dog. No owner. Just a continual build-up of 'presents' for months on end. Then one day – nothing.

Phantoms are known to be migratory and, having flooded an area with shit till the smell becomes unbearable, he or she will then move on to a fresh territory, deliciously unsullied, ready for contamination. To date Phantoms are confined exclusively to parts of the British Isles with dysfunctional cleansing departments.

Dog – Unknown but something massive.
General Appearance – Unknown.
Characteristics – Prodigious producers of pavement fertilizer.
Temperament – Unfailing generous (in their eyes alone).
Body – Unknown.
Gait/Movement – Unknown.
Faults – Anything unable to generate carrier bag-sized poos is deemed a failure.
Least Likely to Own – Poo bags.

Tiny Tantrum

This crossbreed is a curiosity. Rather than finding a dog to share her life with, instead she's drawn to a human child as a substitute canine. She catches the child in and around a maternity hospital when it's a new born pup and then attaches it to a lead. This is strange behavior as the child is much worse at walking, barking and eating than a pooch. Furthermore, unlike a mutt, it refuses to eat its own vomit (expecting someone else to eat it instead).

The child has a very poor sense of smell and has a habit of pooing its pants in a grotesque contraption which involves strapping an absorbent poo bag to its bum at every available opportunity (NB: it can however drag its arse along the carpet as good as any dog). The child is almost impossible to train, always wanting to do what it wants and, as a result, gives this crossbreed Owner its name.

You're most likely to find the Tiny Tantrum in urban areas and it's thought that the cause of this phenomenon is toxic waste pollution turning a normal Owner's brain to syrup, known as 'baby brain'. Remarkably the children appear as well-cared for, if not better looked-after, as their canine peers (remarkable considering how annoying they are), and it should be stressed that this seems not to be a predatory issue.

If a Tiny Tantrum attempts to take your child, it's best to let it do so. Afterwards, simply follow it until it falls into an exhausted sleep, then creep up, cut the lead, and retrieve your child.

Dog – Bizarrely, a small child.

General Appearance – Bedraggled, with a worn coat of blue cagoule and an absence of make-up.

Characteristics – Harassed, totally dominated by her 'pet'.

Temperament – Becomes aggressive easily (Owner), cries easily (Owner and pet), falls asleep easily (Owner and pet).

Body – Impossible to tell through the ill-fitting cagoule, baggy jumper and pyjamas.

Gait/Movement – Slow and cumbersome as the substitute dog totters about like a pissed geriatric.

Faults – If the Tiny tantrum doesn't have massive bags under her eyes then she may not be a crossbreed at all.

Most Likely to Own – Unrealistic ambitions for a quiet night's sleep.

Lovehound

As every spotter knows, Owners can have a propensity to depravity, and so it should come as no surprise that, during the research for this new edition of the Guide, we uncovered a sexual craze that has recently arisen amongst Dog Owners.

Claiming to be 'just going out to walk the dog', breeding pairs of Owner leave their teenage children at home and head for the local country park, taking their unwitting pooch along as cover. Meeting up with like-minded Owners from other areas, they play fetch, roll over and lie down (with each other), whilst the other Owners watch.

Naturally, the Collared Club in no way approves of or condones these actions.

General Appearance – Innocuous, middle aged.
Characteristics – Unfailingly (and sometimes bi) curious and doggedly persistent.
Temperament – Playful. Easily bored. Always looking for some action.
Body – Highly variable.
Gait/Movement – Vigorous, swinging and repetitive from the hips.
Faults – Any sense of shame or embarrassment unlikely to be present in a good example of this crossbreed.
Most Likely to Own – A Ford Mondeo and a copy of *The Curious Incident of Dogging in the Nighttime*.

Glossary of Terms

Action – Movement, the way an Owner walks, trots or sprints yelling after their dog

Amble – A fat trot

Awards – The author of this book is unaware of what awards are

Babbler – An Owner with an inability to shut up about their Dog

Bandy Legs – A common affliction for Owners of dogs with crotch-sniffing behaviour

Beard – Thick, long hair on muzzle and underjaw, best kept trimmed (although over-trimming can result in an Owner being infected with Hipster)

Beaver – Not an Owner, nor a Dog (can be spotted in country parks)

Bitch – An affectionate term used by many male Owners for their breeding partners

Bolting Eye – A lecherous look, characterised by the protruding eyes of many Gun-dogging owners when a Toy walks past

Bossy – An overdeveloped sense of entitlement demonstrated in public places

Breeching – An unfortunate instance when hair is found on the outside of thighs and on back of buttocks, spotted amongst urban Owners with low-slung trousers

Carpals – Bones of the wrist that in Owners are markedly longer in one hand, known as the 'leading hand', caused by too much tugging

Cat-footed – The limp acquired by Owners when their dogs go mad at the sight of a feline

Crabbing – Owner moves with body at an angle to line of travel, usually due to a strong dog on the lead

Cry – The baying of an Owner as their dog vanishes over a rise

Double Coat – Essential for Owners; an outer coat resistant to water, together with an undercoat for warmth

Fancier – A person especially interested in visiting country parks with their dog after the hours of daylight

Feathering – Long fringe of hair on ears or nose that probably cost a hundred quid

Fetch – A bonding experience between Owner and dog, where the dog drops the ball and the Owner must retrieve it

Field Trial – The act of an Owner trying to catch their Dog when off-lead in the countryside

Forceful Action – Strong, driving movement, occasionally involving a rolled-up newspaper

Frogface – An insult

Furrow – Marks in the ground left by Owners when they are attempting to stop a strong, determined dog

Gone to Ground – When the dog vanishes at bath time

Gun-shy – When the dog realises its owner is a poor shot and fears for its own safety

Handler – An Owner who's a bit too touchy-feely for a dog's liking

Hard-mouthed – When an Owner doesn't mince his or her words when calling their dog

Harness – For dog owners interested in the ancient Japanese art of Shibari

Honorable Scars – To be found on the legs of postmen

Inbreeding – A simple equation: w (wealth) x l (land) = i (inbreeding)

Jowls – Found on Ulster Protestants and lazy Owners

Keen – A penetrating expression used by Owners when accused of not collecting their dog's excrement

Leonine – When what an Owner actually has is a Big Cat

Litter – The pile of small, knotted plastic bags that surround park bins, occasionally also found in bushes for no clear reason

Melon Head – An insult

Monorchid – Having only one testicle in the scrotum, such as Hitler

Moult – As the weather heats up in Spring Owners lose layers of clothing

Poke – Where an owner uses the tip of their toe to find out what it is their Dog has brought them

Retrieve – Owners fetching an expensive toy their dog has discarded several hundred yards away

Ruby Eye – The red-tinged look Owner's develop when their Dog is still in the puppy-up-all-night stage

Scent – Blaming the dog for one that slipped out in company

Season – The time for visiting the country park

Shed – The place one's dog is put when returning home after rolling in something dead

Veterinarian – A scourge; to dogs they represent pain and fear, to Owners they represent penury and fear

Wall Eye – How dogs locate a place to pee

Acknowledgements

I'd like to thank the compilers of the Kennel Club's *Illustrated Breeds Standards*, upon which this lampooning relies heavily.

Thanks also to Judith Hastie for her wonderful illustrations, and to the designers at Freight, who have to deal with what many people would put in a plastic bag and leave next to the bin in the park.

Dedicated to the estimable, hilarious, heroic and brave Fi Brook, long may she be.